on drowning a rat

Adrian Flavell

on drowning a rat

PICARO PRESS

Acknowledgements

Poems included in this collection have been previously published in the following: *The Australian*; *Beyond the Rainbow*; *Blue Giraffe*; *Burley*; *The Canberra Times*; *Egg Poetry*; *famous reporter*; *Idiom 23*; *The Independent Weekly*; *LiNQ*; *NSW School Magazine*; *Page Seventeen*; *Polestar Writers Journal*; *Radio 5UV*; *Regime*; *Reid's Magazine*; *Social Alternatives*; *Southern Review*; *Splatter Magazine*; *Tamba*; *Takahe*; *Thirst*; *UQ Vanguard*; *Westerly*; *Woorilla*; *The Write Angle*

With special thanks to Amy Milhinch and Helen Mills

on drowning a rat
ISBN 978 1 921691 66 9
Copyright © text Adrian Flavell 2013
Cover illustration: Helen Mills

First published by Picaro Press 2013

This edition published 2015 by
Picaro Press – an imprint of
GINNINDERRA PRESS
PO Box 3461 Port Adelaide 5015 Australia
www.ginninderrapress.com.au

Contents

on drowning a rat	9
end of an era	10
the freeway	11
the seduction	12
a certain sadness	13
duck season	14
pre-loved	15
outside her room	16
happy hour drinks	17
their last date	18
she chooses	19
the party	20
road kill	21
her sadness	22
caution	23
the domestic	24
his argument	25
her smile	26
her love (x2)	27
ode to a romantic cynic	28
two views of camera	29
confession	30
garden party	31
three approaches to love	34
no corners left	35
the punch	37
a veteran	38
border control / hotel security	39
peak-hour	40
snaps	41

a meagre life	42
over it	43
'no dogs allowed'	44
left alone	45
the intruder	46
outside woolworths	47
good neighbours	48
an accident: the dog's story	50
I knew I needed to get out more…	51
culture	52
the bruise (x2)	53
the victim	54
moon poems	55
the moon	57
mirrors	58
at the edges	59
the author	60
child drowning	61
after the funeral notice	62
on his death	63
a romantic departure	64
the stroke ward	65
in doubt	68
she is alone	70
figs	71
lily	72
pomegranate	73
a new subdivision	74
sunset settles	75
wherever	76
5th world	77
the garage fridge	78

magpies	79
pizza parlour	80
curry	81
mushrooms	82
anchovies	83
sunday dinner	84
keen	85
oysters	86
beyond the beach cliff	87
the lighthouse	88
American River – Kangaroo Island	89
yachts	90
I've seen hell	91
bait	93
squid (1)	95
squid (2)	96
the fish	97
sardines	98
seasonal	99
Darwin	100
waiting for the wet	101
central market	102
the jetty	103
the trawler / Backstairs Passage	104

to Johanna –
for all those years
and these

on drowning a rat

the rat

its back already broken
like too many ceasefires / promises / dreams

is dropped into a bucket

you could have died
with a last meal of choice
but instead you drink
till your lungs burst

like bubbles / balloons
and the skulls of children

too slow to escape the hammer

end of an era

the kookaburra laughs
(forever a smart arse)

to herald break of rain
or a better tomorrow

unaware
that he is the joke

as the cross-sights
settle on his jackass face

one breath from laughter

then the sad crack
of startled feathers
and he's smacked
from the tree

to crazy skydive
the fall from grace

and on the ground

just a thin sneer
of near death

with a half-bent wing
raised in memory

the freeway

skull crushed
with brains punched out
the ears and nose

what was a koala
now spread like
vegemite
across asphalt toast

it was too early
for its last breakfast

as trucks cruised
the inside lane
hoping for hikers

the seduction

the bird

with its eye torn
and hanging
like a cherry

has no choice

but to shuffle
within broken shade
and tremble

to the pleasure of cat

a certain sadness

the parrot calls (out)

calls louder

as rosellas screech past
like an emergency

while a single feather
lifts from the cage

in pale reflection of flight

duck season

the duck
breaks the dam's mirror

shattering
its own reflection

and trailing wave
towards reeds

where years of bad luck

are measured
by both barrels

of twelve-gauge superstition

pre-loved

her dress
was handed down

like advice

and lifted

by the same uncle

whose words warned

    …of boys

    …of cars

    …of unattended drinks

    …of leaning into secrets

where butterflies are trapped
banging against the glass

outside her room

he stood
hands folded
behind his back

like unused bed linen

waiting

for the light
and their love

to go out

happy hour drinks

the half-smile
of a lipstick smudge

edging the glass

suggests

a slug

squashed
while cruising
the length of tongue

their last date

under a peach moon
she peeled him back
to the beginning

skinning his fox of memory

and leaving him
pulp pink

as the foetus

she chooses

after faltering through
the confusion of sex

she chooses
to brood the party fringe

skirts the edges

and sifts towards
the social whirl

to snatch at shadows

as if
stealing wordless speech
is a treachery

of its own

the party

she left him

like an unattended drink –

half empty / lipstick-stained

and serving as an ashtray

road kill

(presumed accident on love's highway)

discarded
like roadkill
she left him

emotional possum
playing dead

startled by headlights

his eyes caught
and running
every wrong way

her sadness

time drifts through
the buttons of her blouse

pain is smudged
as mascara to her eyes

her sadness
drips sticky
to the corners of
conversation

she spreads
her memories thinly
sparingly
as though these were the last

(and she would know)

caution

she treads   too closely
the blade of life

where a slip   either way
opens veins

and deals   blood red
a hand

that can only lose

the domestic

her blood settles

like treacle

on a pancake

his argument

his argument
gives way

like rotting timbers

leaving him marooned
beyond the sanity
of harbour

her smile

her smile
is spreading
like spilt paint

colouring her canvas
of children

for life's exhibition
of mother's image

her love (x2)

(1)

her love drifts
like spider thread
on a distant song

(2)

her love floats
the slipstream
between the silken sighs

ode to a romantic cynic

oh rose
though art
and being such
is a prick

two views of camera

(1)

exposed
like forgotten film

she fixes a grin

in the album
of his life

(2)

she develops

in the dark room

of his heart

a snapshot
of uncertainty

confession

after hearing
his confession

she moved on
from forgiveness

to thread his words
as beads of conscience

and crafted a guilt

to hang sombre around his neck

garden party

she sits
thought hazed

needing
but not believing
the lives of others

grieving for
the shrapnel torn
the shadow hungry

the restless
homeless
helpless situations
of neighbours

locked in panic

to each
her own

for each
her own
draught of wordless poison

bloodletting
wrists opened
like wedding presents

throats gasping
sour-faced recipes

leeches to the heart
draining black the memories

of how
things should have been
may have been
but for the pain

between the promise
and the present

without power
without glory

theirs is the kingdom
where truth
is a litter of puppies

each knocked

nuzzling the hammer that
shatters dog skulls

bitch-barking
boot battered

woman to woman

strays in the street
kept at heel
by puppy whimperings

here
thoughts are traded

hands locked
in hearts journeys

and drinks
passed as sentences

sometimes
women are mended

put back
on the shelf

good as new

the party cools

marital temperatures drop

this/is/the/domestic/ice/age

three approaches to love

(1)

s/he runs into love

reckless

like a dog
at the rail crossing

(2)

he steps into love
with the caution
of his son's first ride

without trainer wheels

(3)

she careers into love

at top speed –

burn outs/doughnuts

it's all good

till she fails
to give way
to her right

no corners left

when words collide
and there are no corners left

for safety's sake

without a hiding place
for your own sake

there's no easy way

where there's smoke
there has to be

whatever burns
has been lit

it sinks
from the skin
and the heart

it creeps

holding on too long
too hard for some

but others slip
slapped around
baby – bashed

watching from the side
whimpering
whingeing

never enough

too often
they're too little
their cries
falling on bruised ears

dribbling on death's door
clinging to the ivy vine
leaping past the window

to a solution
known only
as a blight of memories

an infestation of emotion

a reckoning
where there's nowhere
left to turn

the punch

his nose swells

blood drips
like a second hand

tock – tock – tock

pooling on the lino
in the redness
of careless paint

his nose broken

like the surf
on wild-eyed beaches
where the sea
wrestles its chaos

and the sun buckles
under its own heat

while in hindsight

his misjudged gesture
proving colour
for the casual artist
to blur distinction between
the image and the pain

a veteran

memory sets
as hairspray

or as the sun

crazy skidding
beyond world's edge

border control / hotel security

his grin
was a doorway to refusal

no point asking

more immediate
to slam an elbow
and reduce stupidity
to the shrapnel of broken teeth

peak-hour

crowds

stretch the street

like a sheet
on a new-made bed

snaps

pillow talk   she made phone calls
                     like she made her bed

                     tight and hard
                     with crisp white sentences

                     that left no one
                     expecting emotional parole

domestic forecast   he bore criticism
                     like a storm

                     turned on windscreen wipers
                     and drove through

safety issue   you did me up
                     as a safety belt
                     crossing somewhere
                     between your breasts
                     but clear
                     of the heart

a meagre life

inside: drunk for a fifth day
the man disconnects his world
like a power failure

outside: along the fence line
the dog gleans cat turds
and sucks dead flies
from the window ledge

he's grazed the backyard
to a starvation stubble
and now his bones fold
under an excuse for skin

the outcome: the front door opens
like a drunken mouth
whose breath
has kissed the dead

and in the yard
the landlord shovels the dog
into the wheelie bin

impassive
to the meagre
sigh of life

over it

their love disappeared

like a dog

chasing its fear
of thunder

'no dogs allowed'

'no dogs allowed'

stationed on the gate
like security

but literacy
not being one of their skills

my dogs entered

anyway

left alone

the dog
folds at the door

curling its legs
like ribbons

and wrapping
as a gift
for their return

the intruder

my dog growls

my dogs growl

like stomachs
left empty
far too long

outside woolworths

stitched to the post
like a ribbon of distemper

the dog sighs

its waiting
wearing thin
a canine patience

good neighbours

we heard the shot
and checked over the fence

at first
it was clear

but then the dog came
with its belly on the ground
leaving a red smear
like mosquitoes on a mirror

it looked puzzled

like it didn't know

we look puzzled

because we did

then our neighbour appeared
pulling at the nose
of his old twenty-two

'thing's jammed'
by way of explanation

then he finished the dog
with his rifle butt

and jumped two feet heavy
onto its head

popping an eye
to splat the fence
and causing us to duck

'fuck off'
said our good neighbour

an accident: the dog's story

the dog's snarl
sticks to the tyre

while its body
wrestles the road
in a chaos

of spine and gravel
of bitumen and bone

I knew I needed to get out more…

I knew I needed
to get out more when:

I talked to my dogs
and they answered back

I chased magpies
off the back lawn

I barked at passing cars

I ate the cat's vomit

I cocked my leg
on the rose bush

I used my tongue
instead of a flannel

and I bit the hand
that tried to feed me

culture

like waiting
for the meek
to inherit whatever

no one's waiting
for godot

fuck him

if he can't make it
he could've called

or texted

or tweeted

so the flash mob
could scramble places
on the bench

but no

he's beyond that
up himself

so fuck him

we'll go a burger
at least you can
rely on them

wherever / whenever

without that doubt
of expectation

the bruise (x2)

1.

the bruise spreads
like rancid gossip

its ink wash of anger
swilling beyond family

yet settling
to stain her child

2.

the bruise develops
like a photograph
with shadows
of foreign lands
emerging as honour
out of focus

and needing to kill

the victim

he thrust

and twisted
until his hand
pushed hard
against the belly fat

the steel turned
with the ease
of a door handle

the feet lifted
to tips of toe

blood bubbled
and crept
the corners of mouth

this knife

had cut all ties
with calm and reason

had abandoned courts
and trial procedures

had set him apart

had finished
what his words
could never say

moon poems

(i)

the moon
through mist

lunar dew

laughing
at the lateness

of morning

(ii)

clouds shift
to tilt stars

in cosmic winks

while pearl moon
shucks
its oyster of blackness

(iii)

the moon
lunar laughing

at the conspiracy
of man

whose small step

tripped them
off the edge

to circle
in dangerous worship

and wonder

at the flatness
of earth

the moon

precious moon

orange bead of yesterday

hung low on world's neck
to romance the sleep

and thread love
as jewellery of the night

mirrors

the lake
laps the shore

like a dog

thirsty
from chase

at the edges

the sea

…calm tonight

    for a change

just a soft licking

at the edges

the author

scalping
her memories of love

she lifts their locks

and strands them
between the pages

child drowning

the pool teased
in the casual heat

reflecting lakes
to ocean edges

and

like a bottle
held under water

bubbles of life
broke
on the cruel surface
of a nightmare

after the funeral notice

cards arrive
like migratory birds

all within a few days

coming to roost
within the safety of mailbox

on his death

it wasn't an accident

no – you had to be killed
by your own heart

some reluctant suicide
that you hadn't planned

no beyond blue despair
nor visions of dark-eyed virgins

this edged upon you
and tricked past
the scans and security checks

then detonated

leaving you blood-shocked
and looking for reprieve

a romantic departure

he packed his bags

and tucked his life
into the case

knowing too well

he wouldn't pass security

with a love

that registers
as an incendiary device

the stroke ward

through corridors
turning jackboot
like a compass needle

into lifts
shared with the bikie
dribbling his last memory
into a pooling
of vomit and gang warfare
where the Cherokees
have left him
all but scalped

through other corridors
where families hang
with the inertia of grief
and nurses
spit their words
like food fried too hot

until the stroke ward

here

the folding and flapping of arms
the squawking of seagulls
desperate for the guts

of last night's catch

the old man
with the jumper wrapped
around his head
lies somewhere between
hindu and elephant man
and claims
he could screw
all the nurses
but has forgotten why

then your own father

last bed of the row

like a battery hen
pulling and pecking
at the real
and otherwise

symbol of so much
gone wrong
and more that could have
but for your sacrifice

for learning
to always meet
short of halfway

here

those things
that stopped you
sorting through
the certainty of emptiness

of finding no comfort
within remorse

are still there

you know
what you hold
or let slip

not catch
or capture
on the edge
of a dying man's bed

and watching now
I see a history swelling

rising around you
as an emotional tide

where feelings are
washed over
and left hanging
on the high-water mark

in doubt

like everyone
she must have wanted
diffrent things
at different times

but now
too sad
and alone

the journey
past abandoned fairytales
of being fed lies
and bled to drain
what could be true

in doubt
the journey
through
the body and the pain

the sadness of options
and choices to travel
between lives

she could be so far

she could be so near
to the stranger
in darkness
calling long distance
to crosshatch
the surface
of her changing life

and watching for weakness

she is alone

she is alone

she steps outside
to taste the plum coloured night
whose dark curves
press firm like fruit

she turns arabesque

dips and pirouettes

the soft stroke of wind
teases hair about her face

lifts and licks
around her blouse

from here
she is amongst blue iris
and shadowed
in a dream of daisies

she is alone

I am watching

figs

fleshed
to the fullness
of tongue

to suck
and spit

and fill
the mouth

with salvation

lily

lily as paradox

this lighthouse
with cobra hood

a beacon of sanity
in the craziness of garden

yet left gagging
with a yellow finger
poked down its throat

pomegranate

pomegranate
as placenta
of the fruit bowl

with beads
of birth blood

to suck
and blast
across a drift
of white china

a new subdivision

the crow

stitching between
fallen branches

settles

as a black armband

in memory of tree

sunset settles

sunset settles
as the bloodshot eye
of day's end

the sea
rests an arm
around a bruised coast

from such wreckage
there is a quiet

wherever

bones crack

within the jaws

of my dog

or the hammer

shelling the skull

of a dissident

5th world

seagulls
as tidy scavengers

keep too clean

considering the children
who share the same dump

the garage fridge

the fridge
jerks into life

like medical intervention

or a rabbit
snatched
in the shock of steel

magpies

magpies
as storm troopers
bully their way

through the prism
of rosellas
scattered into flight

gestapo of the bird world

black and white
hard colours
with no movement for grey

they rule here

other birds
seek refuge

displaced from the familiar
like the human cargo

at railway station

pizza parlour

through the rain
and steamed-up window
I saw the guy do his one-man-zorba-dance
flipping his pastry
and finally laying her in
the greased-round-tray

slammed in the oven
and sizzled

and then
the final coffin
of the take-away box

curry

inca of the spices

worth its weight
as gold
for the sacrificial lamb

its eureka
in the kitchen

prompting another rush
to alaska

mushrooms

sheltering spores of discontent
and refuge for sedition

hostile fungus

plotting deceit
in dark and damp cultures

no surprise
for those
who keep company
with shit

anchovies

horse hair of the palate

nautical fur ball

dog hairs
from ocean mats

this bristle fish
that bites
with passion
from the deep

and slow sucks

all juices
from the tongue

sunday dinner

rack of lamb

tortured heretic
of sunday's dinner

basted with rumour

and roasted
in the inquisition
of family

keen

the sea tugs
at the shore

like children

keen to move
on to ice cream

oysters

oysters
shucked
to the taste of sea

wet gasps
of mermaid breathing

soft tissue
of ocean sex

treasures for the sunken

beyond the beach cliff

the hawk

correcting its bank
to the time of sea

scatters pigeons

like confetti
thrown at dawn

the lighthouse

seagulls
hedge the daze
of midday

borrowing the shadow
of a fisherman's net

further out
the lighthouse
with shared colour and size

we wait
for it
to rise and dip
with the throwing of bread

American River – Kangaroo Island

tidal flats yawn
beyond an easy walk

as pacific gulls
work the tide line
at both ends

of the day

yachts

sailing the rim
in the stillness of sun

yachts
are debris
amongst the blueness

unwanted intrusions
crazy yapping
and skitting everyways

like dogs
on a bone

I've seen hell

I've seen hell

well – smelt it first

waiting for petrol
in the cheap day queue

actually – heard it first

heading towards
the intersection
in near peak-traffic
bumper to bumper

the screams
the squeals

        of pain
        of panic

then the smell

shit and fear
in one truck
packed so hard
that body parts
stuck out
like unwanted guests
at a dinner
with too few seats

and that's what I saw

the pig's face
peeling away
into the steel mesh

so that
its eye caught mine

for too long

before it popped
to hang yo-yo

as the lights
changed red

bait

there is a story

that here the cliffs
are eroded by tears

and that he took the child
near where the river
bleeds to sea

snatched by back legs
and stuffed into a hessian sack
like a christmas fowl

while parents fished a tide
that promised and teased
and lured attention
in the casting of dreams

and so he rowed beyond
the insistence of waves
with the sack at his feet

until the darkest water
where black spills to ocean floor

and here
he removed the child
from the bait sack

snapped ankles and wrists
to fold like a present

and then wrapped arms
with a twist
through the cane of his craypot

before the final shove
that lost the gasping mouth
to the swallow of sea

the bones of this story
rattle through our families
and grief rages against
this inkwell ocean
that remains silent
on the writing of lives
and trades secrets for sacrifice

squid (1)

squid
as maritime refugees

shuffling ghosts of the sea

waiting for the wave
as passport to freedom

squid (2)

squid
ripped from the sea

running through his wardrobe
from muddied autumn
to milk of death

then his final defiance

to ejaculate ink
onto the page
of his assassin

the fish

the fish
favours a choreography
dictated by instinct

given that the hook
is ripping
the smile from its face

its moves are
snappy and desperate

there's no subtlety
of form and movement

just a bloodied ballet
of imminent death
and when cooked

a strange taste of dying

sardines

sardines
crammed and crowded

refugee fish

packed for profit
and flavoured with a sauce
too rich for some

seasonal

spring: loose hair
                        collecting herbs
            breast slipping
            out of cambric shirt
                        briskly tucked back
                        with a sprig of thyme

late autumn:
            through the rain
            storing the coming
            winter's wood
                        lichen smudged
                        against leather
            resisting timber
            thrusting itself
            painfully
                        up bitten fingernails

summer:
a) the sadness   b) patches
   of sand castles   of bikini pale
   to last   exposing her breasts
   but one tide   as negatives

Darwin

Darwin
the evolution of place

cyclone – dreaming
its tale of two cities

its flaw
as first line defence

its hostile waters
stretching a coastline

its captured boats
fishing an outlaw tide

its mango – slush of sensibilities

its microwave of the senses

its whispering
from the long grass

waiting for the wet

rhyme for a heatwave

the day sways
in the drifting haze

central market

somewhere
a rising anger

in spanish

younger voices
skidding across generations

blanket bombing
reluctant cities

their civil war declared
amidst the passion of family

and the shopper

reluctant to miss
familial carnage

folds between stalls
like pre-made pastry

the jetty

the jetty
like an unfinished bridge
holds the promise

of a day beyond today
and a step beyond world's end

the trawler / Backstairs Passage

the trawler
is suspended
kite-like

hung somewhere
between sea and sky

shadow puppet
at world's end

silhouette dockyard
dissolving at skyline

its cargo frozen
with gaping mouths

fish snapped
for portside market

and others elsewhere
learning
the mystery of journey
and the menace of arrival

www.ingramcontent.com/pod-product-compliance
Lightning Source LLC
Chambersburg PA
CBHW071010080526
44587CB00015B/2408